Grants for Artists

Grants for Artists

How to find and apply for grants for individuals

Alex Tack

Art should be something that liberates your soul, provokes the imagination, and encourages people to go further.

—Keith Haring

Contents

Start Here

If you picked up this book, you're either a working artist or you aspire to be one. Whether you're teaching in the arts, making your hustle as an artist, or on the road to doing one of those things, I understand where you're coming from.

When I started my career as a videographer, I spent most of my time struggling to balance flexible day jobs, corporate gigs and weekend weddings. It seemed like a never-ending quest to find resources to work on my first love: documentary film. I knew I could hustle with the best of them, but I dreamed of spending more time on my own projects. That's what I had trained for!

Like most working artists, family responsibilities and work obligations kept me from having time to explore my personal projects. Over the years I've spent hours in gripe sessions with other photographers, writers, designers, and creatives over our lack of time and resources. If you can relate, welcome to the club.

Here's how that changed.

I was working as an office assistant for a nonprofit arts organization. The organization was incredibly short staffed, and I was practically working for free. (An arts org with no funding? Hard to believe, I know.)

One afternoon I read about a state-sponsored grant for job training programs. It sounded perfect for a new film program we were putting together. Our city was a hotbed of production activity because of its generous tax credits, and we knew we could get more locals hired with the right job training.

We had the curricula but had no budget for equipment, training space, or marketing the program. Our organization only had four staff members, and we were cramped in a closet-sized office. None of us had ever written a grant before, but we talked it over and knew this program was a good fit for the grant, and it could really help the community.

I volunteered to take a stab at the application. I had done some freelance writing, and I'd written some of the course materials for the program, so I understood our mission.

That decision opened a new opportunity.

If you're worried about your writing skills, you don't need a writing background to apply for grants. You only need the desire to learn the process. You also need to understand your personal mission and be able to explain it to others. We'll take that on in the tips section!

I had been working with the organization for about a year, and I'd gotten pretty comfortable presenting our mission to individual funders. I'd read a few books on fundraising, and I figured it couldn't be that hard to communicate the program's goals in a grant application. Right? I mean, how hard could it be? (As you'll learn in this book, it takes some organization but it's not as hard as you might think.)

Some of you may be starting out where I was. I had never seen a grant application before. I had no clue what we'd need to provide to apply. But I believed in our mission, and I knew the funds would go a long way to helping people in our community learn job skills.

So, I got started.

Here's the real talk: Grant proposals can be intimidating. They can be complicated. And there are usually a ton of instructions that must be followed to the letter. If you think there's a huge pile of money out there and you're only one trying to get a piece of it ... well, think again. Competition for grant funding is fierce, especially for individuals seeking creative grants to support their work.

But that doesn't mean it isn't possible! It is doable. It just means you need to do your research, understand what people are asking for, and learn how to present your project in a way that gets people excited to support you.

It also helps if you have a personal mission statement that aligns with whoever is giving out the funds! But we'll get into that later in this book.

Ready for some more real talk? You can definitely figure it out. You just need a little patience and some willingness to follow instructions and explain the value of your work.

You may be wondering, how did our first grant attempt go? After I read and re-read the application instructions many times, we spent a couple of weeks gathering all the information they asked for. I got to work writing the grant narrative. The "narrative" is just the story of your project. It explains in a clear and engaging way why they should support you.

During the writing process, I called the funding office's phone number a few times to ask questions and talk to the grant coordinator to make sure I was providing all the necessary information. They were actually very helpful and willing to answer questions, which I wasn't expecting. Yes, you can and should talk to the grant coordinators and ask questions! We'll cover when and how to reach out in the tips section.

In the end, we were awarded a grant that was large enough to help us launch the program. It didn't cover the whole thing, but it was enough to get us to the initial launch. It felt like a huge success, and it made me want to keep applying for grant funding.

From then on, I learned everything I could about the grantmaking process. I started applying for any grants we seemed to have a shot at. I even got comfortable reaching out to other organizations for in-kind support and non-monetary gifts that helped our mission.

As an individual artist, you won't have as many large grant opportunities as nonprofit organizations, but there are a host of residencies and other in-kind support programs available for creatives. (In-kind support is when someone gives you something of value, usually in exchange for mentioning them in promotional materials or by acknowledging them in another way. For example, you might receive 20 hours of studio time in exchange for a social media shoutout. These agreements are unique to each artist and donor.)

Once I got embedded in the grant world, I started helping friends apply for individual artist grants. Most of my friends are writers and photographers, so I found myself working mainly on individual grant proposals for creatives. However, individual grants exist for the sciences and many other disciplines. The principles in this book apply to any type of grant writing, even scholarship applications! The tips and resources in this book can be used by people outside of the creative field to help them write better scholarship and grants applications, even if they're not looking for arts funding.

More real talk for you: Grant proposals are competitive. Our organization didn't win everything we applied for. Not even close. In some cases, our mission didn't align closely enough with the donors, and in others we weren't a good fit for that round of funding, but we were invited to apply again. While experiencing both success and rejection, I learned a lot about what funders are looking for and how creatives can make the case for support.

I get asked a lot whether there's a ton of free money out there for artists. Sadly, there isn't a secret vault out there filled with cash. Especially for the arts. But that doesn't mean there isn't any funding at all ... there is.

Sometimes people will ask me if they can "make a living" going from grant to grant to grant. I personally haven't seen that happen. However, I have seen people get multiple personal films, book projects, and gallery shows funded. I also know people who won residencies to attend a creative retreat or to spend a month at an artists' colony, so they have uninterrupted time to finish their latest project. Never underestimate the power of free room and board and the gift of time!

So, grants are out there. If you're working on a project that you're passionate about, there are organizations out there doing everything they can to help support artists who are serious about their craft.

I can't guarantee you'll win every proposal, but I wrote this book to give you the direction and advice I wish I had when I first started applying for grants.

Here's what you'll learn in this book:

The first part of this book is a basic overview of what a grant is (and isn't) and how grants for individuals are different from grants for organizations.

The second part contains tips and advice for grant

applications, including how to narrow down and articulate your personal mission.

And finally, you'll find a jumping off point to start your Grant seeking journey. The resources section has information on where to find grant opportunities and links to application information for some of the larger grant opportunities in the United States.

Keep in mind funding agencies may change their scope and guidelines, so always check for the latest information on their websites.

By the end of this book, you should feel more comfortable with researching, writing and submitting your own grant proposals. I've included links to online resources wherever possible, but the online world is constantly changing so you may need to do a little digging if a resource goes inactive.

I included as many free courses as I could find (as a fellow artist and nonprofit worker!), but some of the resources are subscription based or require a fee.

As for my personal grant writing journey, I found an unexpected career helping people fund their projects. I still make short films, but I ended up embracing my passion as a grant writer. I hope this resource helps you spend more time furthering your passion, in whichever medium you work!

Get to Know Grants

What Are My Options?

For creative professionals in fields like writing, illustration, photography, acting, and others, grant funding can be a game-changer. One of the most challenging aspects of performing your craft is finding the time and resources to get your projects across the finish line. (Unless you have a deep-pocket patron or you're independently wealthy!)

Grant funding won't give you the financial freedom to sail the world without care, but it can help you make progress on a project. It can also provide professional contacts and help you build your portfolio. If you're on the fence about whether to put in the effort to learn grant writing skills, here are some of the main reasons it can be worth it in the long run.

Financial Support

Yes, it's obvious, but grant funding provides a valuable source of financial support for creative professionals. Whether you're embarking on a new project, seeking resources for ongoing research and development, or trying to wrap up post-production or publication, grants can provide financial backing to take the next step in your project.

Some grants are earmarked to cover specific expenses such as equipment, materials, travel, production costs, and even living expenses in some cases. Others are open-ended and have minimal restrictions. This extra help frees you from financial constraints and allows you to fully immerse yourself in your creative work.

Even if you don't win a grant after applying, the process helps you explore different types of financial support. You learn the language of arts funding, and you may even come up with creative ways to approach individual patrons!

Skills Development

Grant funding offers creative professionals the freedom to explore new ideas and experiment with their craft. Unlike traditional employment or client-driven projects, grants provide the opportunity to pursue personal projects and take artistic risks. With grant support, you can delve into uncharted territories, push boundaries, and nurture innovative concepts that might not receive backing through other means.

Residencies are another way for artists to get support, and the application process is usually very similar to grant applications. We'll cover the basics of residencies in the next chapter, but know this option is out there. Some residencies require you to create work around a theme or to teach workshops, which can help you explore your craft more deeply.

One of the most valuable assets you gain from grants and residencies is time. Awards that include time at a retreat or an artist-in-residence appointment often come with dedicated periods for focused work, allowing creatives to have time specifically for their artistic development. This uninterrupted time can lead to creative breakthroughs, refined skills, and honing your artistic voice.

Access to Professional Networks and Mentorship

Many grant programs offer networking opportunities and access to industry professionals and mentors. These connections can be invaluable in expanding your creative circle, forging collaborations, and gaining guidance from experienced individuals in your field. Engaging with a network of fellow artists, mentors, and grant administrators can provide valuable insights, support, and potential career opportunities. Whether you are awarded a grant or not, you'll start to expand your circle of contacts by getting to know people at arts organizations.

Visibility, Recognition, and Credibility

Being awarded a grant carries a stamp of credibility and recognition. Being a grant recipient not only enhances your artistic reputation but also opens doors to new opportunities. Grants can elevate your profile, leading to increased visibility among peers, potential clients, publishers, and galleries. The recognition and validation that come with being awarded a grant can serve as a steppingstone to further success in your creative career.

Applying for grants, even if not awarded, is a valuable learning experience. The process of crafting a compelling grant proposal forces you to articulate your artistic vision, goals, and strategies. It sharpens your communication and project management skills, providing a platform for self-reflection and refinement of your creative practice. Each application serves as an opportunity for growth, honing your ability to convey your artistic intentions effectively.

If you've told yourself there's no reason to try because it's too much work, or it's too difficult – reconsider those doubts. Even for artists who don't win awards, crafting their artistic narrative for a grant application has the power to transform their professional journey. When you get clear about your vision and your goals, you start to hone your creative focus and trajectory.

When you embrace the opportunities presented by grant writing, seek out suitable funding options, and invest the time and effort into crafting compelling proposals, these applications can be the catalyst that amplifies your creative pursuits, expands your horizons, and unlocks new artistic possibilities.

What's the difference between grants, residencies, contest prizes, and fellowships?

Before we get into the weeds of how to apply, let's address a common confusion: What's the difference between a grant and other kinds of awards? If you open any website or magazine geared toward artists, you'll probably find a thick section of ads for contests, residencies, and fellowships. What's the difference between these awards, and which ones are best for you?

Let's start with some quick and dirty definitions.

Grants

Grants are financial awards provided by organizations like family foundations, government agencies, or philanthropic groups. They are typically given to individuals or nonprofits to support programming, initiatives, or research that aligns with their mission.

Grant opportunities are available in many disciplines, including arts, sciences, education, and social services. Unlike other types of awards, grants usually involve a complex proposal-based application process that requires applicants to provide an outline of their project, budget, and anticipated outcomes.

There are typically guidelines around how the money can be used, and grant recipients are expected to report on their progress. (Yes, you're usually asked to generate a report showing the positive impact the grant had on your project! These are generally simple to create, so don't worry too much about reporting.)

Grants are ideal for individuals who seek funding to support long-term projects, particularly when the project aligns with the funding organization's mission.

Residencies

Ever dreamed of spending two weeks at an outdoor retreat focused entirely on your latest project? Residencies may be for you. They offer artists, writers, and other creatives an opportunity to live and work in a dedicated space for a specific period. It could be something as simple as a season at an urban coworking space or a few weeks at a country farm.

Residencies can be highly competitive because they provide artists with uninterrupted time and space to focus on their craft. They often come with amenities like dedicated studio space, living accommodations, and sometimes stipends or material support. Residencies can be found in all kinds of locations around the world, from urban centers to rural retreats. Artists benefit from solitude and the opportunity to engage with a community of fellow creatives.

Explore residencies when you're looking for focused time and an inspiring environment to develop your artistic practice or complete a specific project.

Contests

Contests, sometimes referred to as competitions, are events where participants submit their work for evaluation by a panel of qualified judges. Contests are open in various fields, including writing, photography, visual arts, and artistic entrepreneurship. Participants compete with one another to win prizes, recognition, or publication opportunities.

Judging criteria may include originality, skill, creativity, and adherence to specific guidelines. Contests offer individuals the chance to gain exposure, showcase their talent, and potentially secure awards or recognition.

Participate in contests can be beneficial for those seeking validation, exposure, and opportunities to connect with industry professionals.

Fellowships

Fellowships are prestigious opportunities typically awarded by academic institutions and large, well-known philanthropic organizations to provide financial support, mentorship, and professional development to individuals. They are usually awarded to individuals participating in advanced study programs or research projects that further the field and create individual career enhancement.

Fellowships are most often found in universities, research institutions, government agencies, or nonprofit organizations dedicated to research. They can span various fields, including academia, scientific research, arts, and public service. Fellows are typically selected based on their achievements, potential, and alignment with the fellowship program's goals. Fellows often receive financial stipends, access to resources, mentorship, and networking opportunities.

Fellowships are well-suited for individuals seeking concentrated periods of study, research, or career advancement in a supportive and intellectually stimulating environment.

The information in this book is geared toward grants, but there are benefits to winning contests, residencies, and fellowships, too. The application tips apply to any of these opportunities, and some of the larger residency and non-grant awards for artists are included in the resources section of this book.

Choosing the Right Path

When considering whether to pursue grants, fellowships,

residencies, or any other opportunity, assess your goals, needs, and priorities. Grants are suitable for those with well-defined projects that require substantial funding. Residencies offer an immersive environment for creative exploration and focused work. Contests provide opportunities for recognition and exposure in a competitive setting. Fellowships are designed to advance education, research, or professional growth with financial support and mentorship.

Ultimately, the choice on where to put your application time depends on your specific aspirations, the stage of your career or project, and the resources you require. Consider the alignment between your goals and the opportunities offered by each type of award. Consider the time commitment, financial support, mentorship, networking potential, and then get to applying!

What kind of grants exist for individuals?

With the overview of different opportunities out of the way, let's get into the weeds of grants specifically. And let's be real: You've probably been hustling for most of your career. You work hard to create and promote your art, whether it's photography, multimedia, poetry or that novel you've been plugging away at for years. No one needs to tell you that being an artist, while creatively fulfilling, is a challenging and sometimes thankless career – especially if you have a day job and family responsibilities tugging at you every day.

For most artists, money is usually an issue. Even if you've found ways to monetize online or by selling in person, very few people are making it rain with their art. For most creatives, it's challenging to stay motivated when you pour so much energy into your work and receive so little compensation in return. (If there's any compensation at all!) Not to mention the constant questioning: Will this ever lead to anything, or should I give up and focus on a day job?

If you've managed to become a successful freelancer, there's a good chance you're so busy hustling don't have a lot of time to pursue your original passions. Working in the field you love is a blessing, especially if you're teaching or coaching others, but a grant would help provide time, space, and funding to work on your artistic achievements.

As an artist, we all have natural fears about balancing the artistic and business sides of our work. And these concerns point to a natural conclusion: You need to explore all possible funding options. You need support for the art you care about, and that's where grants for artists come in. Of course, that's easier said than done, which is why we're going through this crash course.

Grants for Institutions vs. Individuals

Before you start applying, let's understand what types of grants are available to individuals. There are two main types of grants: those for individuals and those meant for organizations or institutions. The difference may seem self-explanatory, but here's a snapshot of the difference:

Institutions: These grants are provided to formal institutions such as nonprofits, educational bodies, associations, etc. While one individual can apply for, receive, and manage an organization's grant, they are doing so on behalf of the institution. This is great to know if you work for someone else and you want to help your organization get a grant, but as a freelancer or individual artist this type of grant is not a good option for you. You won't even be considered if a grant is earmarked for an organization, no matter how worthy your project may be.

Individuals: An individual grant is for one person to be put toward their project. The grant will have specifications for who can apply and how it can be used. If awarded, you must conform to the specifications of the grant and any promises you made when applying for it. In a nutshell, this means you have to use the funding the way you say you'll use it. And you'll follow up with whoever awarded you the grant to make sure you used it toward your project and didn't use the money for a vacation to Tahiti or something. If you receive an ongoing, or multi-year grant, you'll need to achieve the milestones outlined in the grant or risk losing it.

It is possible to get multi-year funding as a freelance artist, but it's more likely you'll get a one-time grant, so make sure to use the money wisely and portion it out to meet your needs. Also, if you're awarded a grant, be sure to check with an accountant about your individual tax situation. In the past, grants were not typically taxable. But tax laws change each year, and you don't want to receive a bill from the IRS and not have the money to pay for it. If your award is taxable, remember to set aside some funds for Uncle Sam.

Granting Agencies

Now that we've had an overview of the difference between grants for organizations and grants for people like you and me, there are several types of organizations that provide grants for individuals. These can include:

State and Local Arts Councils

Most state and local government agencies dedicate money to arts funding each year. In fact, if your city has a lot of tourism, there's a good chance a portion of your hotel and convention taxes go specifically toward arts and humanities grant programs. These grants are awarded to artists living and working in the city or region. They may award grants or hold competitions for local artists to help fund:

- Art supply expenses
- Preparing for a gallery show
- Securing studio space
- Providing art for a municipal building (for example, a library or city hall)

Local municipalities may also put out a Request for Proposal (RFP) to start an art program or to provide art for a park or city exhibition. RFPs will generally be found on the city or county website mixed among other requests like tree trimming services or engineering services, so they may require some digging to find.

The top ten states (by grant amount awarded annually) are listed in the Resources section of this book. If your state isn't on the list, you can always search the internet for your state or city's arts council. Most will have a website, or at minimum an office or contact person listed within city hall or the state house.

Federal Grants

If you can make a strong case for why your work provides a

public service or otherwise helps people in your community, you may qualify for a federal arts grant. The federal government has stringent eligibility requirements, so make sure to take the time to establish your eligibility upfront. Otherwise, you may end up wasting a lot of valuable time filling out applications that won't go anywhere.

Nonprofit organizations are more likely to receive federal funding, but it is possible for individuals to get their proposals accepted as well. Never dismiss an opportunity just because it seems challenging!

Private Foundation Grants

A private foundation is a privately held organization, usually a family foundation, dedicated to helping a particular cause. They are often managed by families with a certain favored cause, and as such, many offer grants to individuals. These foundations may give money for a wide range of reasons, including:

- Belonging to a particular ethnicity or religion around which the organization is founded.
- Coming from a particular background, such as single parents, survivors of abuse or former members of the military.
- Makers of a specific type of art, such as contemporary or multimedia.
- An artist's willingness to give something of value to the foundation in return, such as teaching time or original artwork.
- Educational advancement of the artist, or education grants such as funding PhD research.

Private foundations often have subjective requirements around funding. Don't be afraid to speak with a member of the organization and ask about their preferences and what would help make you a better candidate for receiving the grant.

Corporate Grants

Most companies set aside grant funding as part of their charitable giving efforts. The larger the organization, the more likely they will have a charitable grants program. Sometimes your own company will offer funding or sabbatical time off for personal projects. Check with your human resources department to find out if that's an option.

However, you'll often be looking to outside organizations that have a mission to support the arts. It can sometimes be a challenge to find corporate grant applications, but you can find out more about a company's specific requirements by speaking with or emailing the department that manages charitable giving for the company. Charitable giving information will usually be listed somewhere on the website or in annual reports.

Professional Organizations

Professional organizations, such as writers' associations or painters' societies, are highly motivated to support artists in their field. Depending on the size and mission of the organization, they may offer annual grants for individual artists. You can find out about their artist support efforts on their respective websites.

No matter where you find an opportunity, remember, if you aren't awarded a grant on your first try, you can always apply again. Work on improving and refining your application (be sure to read the tips in section two of this book!) and try again during the next round of applications. Grants aren't a one-shot deal, they're just one part of a long-term funding strategy.

What are umbrella organizations?

There's one more consideration before we jump into the nuts and bolts of writing your grant narrative. You may have heard the term "umbrella organization" in relation to grant awards. You may even see it on applications. Let's demystify what an umbrella organization is and when you may need to work with one.

An umbrella organization, also known as a fiscal sponsor or fiscal agent, is a nonprofit organization that provides support to individuals engaged in charitable or artistic activities. This can include administrative, financial, and legal advice, as well as general mentorship and guidance. These organizations act as a bridge between the grant funder and the individual artist, and they facilitate the receipt and management of grant funds.

What does all that mean in simple terms? There are some funding institutions that will only grant awards to individuals if they have a fiscal sponsor listed in their application. You might also see this called a "fiscal agent," but fiscal sponsorship is more commonly used. The term umbrella organization goes in and out of fashion, but it refers to the fact your grant exists under the "umbrella" of a larger nonprofit.

When you're awarded a grant that requires you to have fiscal sponsorship, the funds are sent to the umbrella organization—your fiscal sponsor—who then forwards the award to you (minus an administrative fee).

In exchange for this sponsorship, they typically assist with the reporting requirements and serve as an overall guide for the individual during the grant term. They will usually help keep the paperwork on the up-and-up from award through final project reporting. Verify this before working with a fiscal sponsor, though, because some organizations will only handle the money and it's up to you to fulfill any reporting requirements.

You may be asking yourself, why do I need a middleman to handle the money? It can help a lot if you're new to the grants world because they'll usually have someone available who can answer questions and help with the logistics.

When do you need to work with a fiscal sponsor or umbrella organization? The glib answer is whenever the application states you do, but there are also other circumstances where it could benefit you:

Nonprofit Status Requirement
The most common reason people partner with an umbrella organization is to access grants that are restricted to nonprofit organizations only. If you are an individual artist without non-profit status, partnering with an umbrella organization that holds 501(c)(3) tax-exempt status allows you to access grants reserved for nonprofits.

The umbrella organization serves as the recipient of the grant funds and ensures compliance with the legal and financial reporting requirements. Under these agreements, you'll need to discuss the project parameters and work out all the details with the nonprofit before you apply. Organizations will have different requirements, including the amount of management fees and types of assistance offered. Some may even help with the grant application; it depends on the arrangement they've made with the artist.

Administrative and Financial Support

Working with an umbrella organization can remove some of the administrative burdens associated with grant management. They might handle tasks such as financial management, bookkeeping, and reporting, allowing the artist to focus on their creative work. Umbrella organizations can provide a structure for project budgets, expense tracking, and maintaining financial accountability, which can be particularly helpful for larger grants with complex financial requirements. Many artists aren't known for their accounting skills (shocking, I know), and working with a fiscal sponsor can be very helpful whether it's required by the granting agency or not.

Credibility and Trust

Grant funders often view these partnerships as a sign of credibility and trust. Collaborating with a reputable, established fiscal sponsor can enhance the perceived professionalism and legitimacy of your project. This can be particularly helpful when applying for grants from major foundations or government agencies where competition is fierce and reporting requirements can be complex. When partnering with a fiscal sponsor, look for one that has a lot of experience working with individual artists. Their advice and guidance may prove invaluable.

Fiscal Sponsorship Opportunities

Some organizations offer fiscal sponsorship programs that go beyond grant management. These programs provide artists with long-term support, including allowing them to receive tax-deductible donations, providing access to a wider range of grants, and benefiting from the organization's resources and network. Fiscal sponsorship can help artists build relationships with donors and expand their fundraising opportunities.

You can approach organizations for fiscal sponsorship even if you aren't currently seeking a grant. Most organizations that offer this type of program will have eligibility requirements listed on their website.

Shared Resources and Networking

On a related note, these organizations can provide access to shared resources, such as studio space, equipment, supplies, and educational opportunities. Organizations that provide fiscal sponsorships often foster a community of artists and provide networking opportunities, collaboration events, and professional development opportunities. Being part of these communities can offer valuable connections, mentorship, and exposure to new work opportunities.

Working with an umbrella organization is not mandatory for all individual artists seeking grants, but it can offer significant advantages in some situations. When considering whether this is right for you, evaluate the specific requirements and benefits of the grants you are applying for. Is fiscal sponsorship necessary to meet eligibility criteria? Would the additional support provided by an organization align with your long-term artistic goals?

Each artist's journey is unique, so the decision to work with a fiscal sponsor should be based on your individual objectives. Weigh the potential advantages and make an informed choice that maximizes your grant-seeking ability while aligning with your vision and aspirations.

Application fees & avoiding scams

There is one more thing to consider before you start the grant seeking journey: *How much is this going to cost?*

Years ago, application fees were few and far between. In fact, many government and university programs had no application fees at all (and some still don't). However, over the years many organizations have been flooded with more and more applicants while their budgets got tighter and tighter. Application fees are common now, so don't be surprised if you're asked to pay a fee to apply. (I'm referring to fees in the $10 to $30 range, beware of astronomical amounts.)

Choose wisely when deciding where to put your application time and resources! Fees will add up when you're applying for several opportunities, and there are plenty of fly-by-night and less reputable operations that make the majority of their money from application fees.

If you want to know whether an application fee looks legit, a good place to start is to look at the ratio of application fee to award amount. If the organization charges $20 or more to apply and they award a few hundred dollars total, do the math. They may be pocketing a lot more than they're giving away.

That's not to say you shouldn't apply, or that those awards are "bad," but use some critical thinking before sending that fee. Unfortunately, scammers abound in the grant seeking world. Here are some warning signs of scams and how to avoid being swindled.

Advanced Fee Scams

Legitimate grants have a website or printed material that contains all the information you need to apply. They will also provide an easy way for you to ask questions, and it's free to reach out to someone during the application process. Many larger granting organizations will even offer an information session where you can attend a meeting and ask questions in person or by video—for free.

Advance fee scams claim to be grants or residencies, but they require you to pay a fee to access application information or ask questions. This is separate from an application fee; this is a fee charged just to access information.

Avoid getting sucked into these scams by walking away from any "grant" opportunity that requires an upfront fee just to view the application or ask questions.

Guaranteed Grants

Beware of any opportunity that "guarantees" you'll win a grant. Legitimate grants are based on merit and a competitive application process. There's no such thing as guaranteed free money, so be cautious of any email or letter that announces you've just been chosen for a guaranteed grant.

Just like those notorious Nigerian princes looking for someone to help them cash their inheritance, these scams start with a communication from an official-sounding person or organization announcing you've been selected for a special guaranteed grant or other cash award.

Once you respond or fill out the enclosed form, you'll be asked for a "processing fee" and they may try to get your bank account information for "direct deposit."

It's easy to get caught up in the excitement of thinking you've been selected for an award. These companies know this, and they prey on people's dreams of success. This scam has been around for decades for a reason—it often works. Be wary any time you find out you've won something you didn't apply for. And keep your banking info to yourself. Of course, that's good life advice in general!

Impersonating Legitimate Grants

This scam is sometimes used with the "guaranteed grant" ploy. This is when a company pretends to be a legitimate grant by having a similar name and logo as a legit award. It confuses people who may not be familiar with the nonprofit world. The name "sounds familiar" so people subconsciously trust it without investigating it as much as they should.

In some cases, you may be approached directly like the guaranteed grant scam. But more commonly, a company will set up a website and provide "grant" information that looks very much like a legit foundation or granting agency.

The site is used to collect people's personal information and a fee, but they're not actually awarding any grants. If you're not sure whether the website you're visiting is a legitimate grant site or not, take the time to check them out.

Visit Cherity Navigator (found at cheritynavigator.org) to find out if they're a rated nonprofit organization. You can also check the Better Business Bureau (at bbb.org) and look for any complaints. The IRS has a searchable database of all tax-exempt organizations, so you can also check if they're listed there. Visit apps.irs.gov/app/eos to search the tax database.

Nailing the Process

Tips for Successful Applications

Now that you've got a working knowledge of what grants are (and aren't), let's talk about how to improve your chances of getting to the final round of consideration. Writing a grant proposal can feel intimidating, and it often feels strange to promote your project, no matter how hard you may work on your craft. If writing isn't your strong suit and you feel overwhelmed by the application requirements, it can seem daunting to create so much text. Talk about every high school English nightmare coming back to haunt you!

Not to worry, though. You can, and will, get through the process. This section will help walk you through the steps to creating a compelling narrative and presenting your project in the best light. You can always have a friend or coworker look over your application for any grammar errors or inconsistencies. You can also hire a copy editor on sites like Fiverr or Upwork. Don't let anxiety over writing stand in your way – there are plenty of resources out there to help you polish the proposal language once you've nailed down these basics.

Tip one: Craft a compelling mission statement

If you've gone through an academic visual arts program, you are probably familiar with writing an artist's statement. It is one of the core activities you participate in as a fine arts student. However, creatives in other disciplines may not be as familiar with this concept. So, in a nutshell, your artist statement is the theory and driving force behind your practice. It's the "why" that motivates your art and what moves you to create.

As a new grant writer, one of your crucial goals is providing a clear and compelling mission statement. It's one of the primary elements that grantors look at when evaluating grant application narratives. Your mission statement not only defines the purpose and values of your project, but it also serves as a guidepost that helps others understand and contextualize your work. To create an effective and compelling mission statement, let's walk through the process of identifying and articulating your project. This foundational exercise will help you create a north star for your grant-seeking journey.

If you prefer worksheets, you'll find a mission statement worksheet at the end of the book. It's a slightly shorter version of the following process. It may be tempting to jump straight to the shorter worksheet, but the work you do in these steps will help you refine your ideas and build better grant narratives.

Reflect on Your Core Values

Start by reflecting on your core values. What principles are at the heart of your work? Consider the beliefs, passions, and driving forces that led you to begin this project or to pursue your creative endeavors in general.

Ask yourself: What impact do I want to make? What values do I want to uphold? This introspective process will provide a solid foundation for your mission statement.

Exercise:

Set a timer for ten minutes and brainstorm all the reasons you do what you do. What legacy are you building? How does your work help others? Let your thoughts flow! Write down any ideas that come to you and expand on them as needed.

When the timer is finished, look over what you wrote and pick out any themes or goals that stand out to you as particularly important.

Define Your Target Audience and Goals

Identify the target audience or the community you aim to serve through your artistic work. Consider the specific needs, challenges, or aspirations of this audience. How do you hope to help them, or how do you wish to inspire them?

Next, define your goals—both the short-term and long-term

outcomes you hope to achieve. How will your work contribute to the betterment of your target audience? What about the broader community? Clearly outlining your audience and goals will help you refine your mission statement.

Exercise:

Again, set the timer for ten minutes and go to town with these questions. Think about the people you hope to reach, and how you'd like to reach them. What is the change you want to be in the world?

Identify Strengths and Opportunities

Here's where you gain a comprehensive understanding of what sets you apart from others in your field. Identify both the areas where you excel and the areas where you can improve and overcome blind spots. Why do you want to know these things? Because there's a very good chance the application is going to ask you what makes you different, and you want to articulate what makes you the best person to use those grant funds. You also want to know what areas you need to improve in—and then improve those things—so you're better prepared to confidently build your narrative. This analysis will make you an overall better candidate.

Exercise:

Set that timer and explore the skills that can be leveraged to further your mission. Also explore potential challenges that may hinder your progress.

Draft One: Refine Key Ideas

Now that you have a clear sense of your values, audience, goals, and personal skills analysis, it's time to craft key phrases, ideas, and words that capture the essence of your mission statement. Emphasize clarity, conciseness, and authenticity. Start with broad statements. You'll refine them to be more specific and impactful in the next step, but for now, paint with a broad brush. Aim for a mission statement that is memorable, inspiring, and aligns with the purpose you've identified.

Here is an example of this first broad draft:

My artistic journey is driven by a mission to nurture creative expression that transcends boundaries and connects hearts.

Through my work, I aim to capture emotions, tell stories, and inspire a deeper understanding of the human experience. My art serves as a catalyst for conversations and connections, fostering a world where diverse perspectives and voices are celebrated. I'm dedicated to expanding my artistic horizons and sharing my passion with the world, one brushstroke at a time.

Craft a Concise Statement

Using the insights gained from the previous steps, begin crafting a more concise mission statement that can be summed up in one or two sentences. You can use the longer version as a launching point and just edit it down or take the same themes and craft a whole new sentence.

Your mission statement is a clear and concise statement that defines who you are, what you do, and whom you serve. Avoid jargon and overly complex language; instead, strive for simplicity and clarity. Consider seeking feedback from colleagues, mentors, or trusted advisors to refine and strengthen your mission statement.

Here are a couple of examples:

Example one: I craft art to ignite conversations about history and human connections in my hometown of Macon, Georgia. Through my work, I aim to challenge perspectives and inspire a shared journey of reflection and growth.

Example two: My art celebrates the beauty of imperfection in nature and life. With my uptown neighborhood as a backdrop, I capture fleeting moments that stir emotions and encourage viewers to find solace and inspiration in the ordinary.

Revise Regularly

Your mission statement is not in stone. As you evolve, your mission may also evolve. Regularly review and revise your mission statement to keep it relevant and accurately reflecting your work. Share your mission statement with people that you trust and ask them to help you spot any areas where you could be clearer.

Tip two: Create a grants calendar

For creative professionals, grant funding or being awarded

an artist residency can carry artistic projects past the finish line and propel career development. However, managing multiple grant applications and associated deadlines can quickly become overwhelming.

That's where a grants calendar comes in handy. It's a way to keep yourself organized and on track to hit deadlines throughout the year. Let's walk through the process of creating a calendar to help you stay organized, meet deadlines, and maximize your chances of securing funding.

Start with Research

How will you know which opportunities to pursue? Put on your research hat. The first step in setting up your calendar is conducting research to identify the grant opportunities relevant to your project or creative field. Explore the resources provided in the next section of the book and make a list of potential grants. Take note of eligibility criteria, funding priorities, and application requirements for each grant. A good way to do this is to simply bookmark each grant application site and save the links to a "grants" folder in your browser.

Determine Your Calendar Format

Choose a calendar format that will work for you. This could be a digital calendar like your default smartphone calendar, a calendar app where you can set deadline reminders, a custom spreadsheet, or even a physical planner that you update each year. You want something where you can easily track deadlines, contact information, submission requirements, and any notes or reminders that will keep you on track. The goal is to create an easy, centralized system that keeps you organized and can be updated as needed.

There's a sample version of a grant calendar at the end of this chapter, but you can also simply add each grant's deadline and a link to their application page on your smartphone calendar.

Capture Grant Deadlines

Record the application deadlines for each grant opportunity on your calendar. Include both major grants and smaller niche grants that might align with your work. Be sure to account for any specific submission timeframes or recurring opportunities throughout the year. Consider setting reminders well in advance of deadlines to allow ample time for preparation and revision.

Create a Timeline

Develop a timeline for each grant application to guide your progress. Break down the application process into smaller tasks and assign deadlines for each task. This could include research-ing, outlining your proposal, gathering supporting materials, and seeking feedback. By creating a timeline, you can manage your workload effectively and avoid last-minute rushes.

Prioritize and Strategize

Consider the time and effort required for each grant applica-tion. Prioritize your applications based on the potential impact, alignment with your goals, and feasibility of completing them within the given timeframe. Strategize by balancing larger grants that require more extensive proposals with smaller grants that can offer quicker turnaround times. Remember that each appli-cation is an opportunity to refine your skills and articulate your artistic vision.

Track Progress and Follow-up

Regularly update your grants calendar to track the progress of your applications. Note the status of each application, such as "in progress," "submitted," or "awarded/rejected." Record any follow-up actions required, such as sending additional materials or confirming receipt of your application. This helps you stay or-ganized and ensures that you don't miss any essential steps in the process.

Stay Informed and Adapt

Stay informed about any changes or updates to grant oppor-tunities throughout the year. Subscribe to newsletters, follow social media accounts of relevant organizations, and join artist communities to stay up to date with new funding opportunities, workshops, and networking events. Be open to adapting your grants calendar as needed to incorporate new opportunities that arise.

Creating a grants calendar is a valuable tool for meeting deadlines and tracking your applications. It helps you organize application dates, create a timeline, and track your progress, which can increase your chances of success. Remember to stay proactive, seek feedback, and refine your applications each time you start a new one. Maintaining a grants calendar not only helps you manage your applications effectively, but also provides a clear roadmap so you don't waste time or miss opportunities.

Tip three: Connect with the grant's mission

Grants and residencies are competitive. In order to stand out in a packed field of applicants, one of the most effective things you can do is ensure that your grant narrative aligns with the mission and goals of the funding organization. If you want to get past the first round of screening, your application should clearly connect with the grant's mission. Here's why it matters and how to make sure you're communicating this connection well.

The Power of Alignment

Connecting with the grant's mission isn't just a formality; it's a strategy that demonstrates you understand the organization and you'll produce work that enhances their reputation. Funders aren't just looking to financially support projects. They also want to champion projects that resonate with their values and goals. If you think about it from their perspective: They don't just want to cut a check. They want to know their money is making a real-world difference and impacting people's lives.

When your grant application aligns with their mission, it demonstrates that you have taken the time to understand the funder's priorities and you are genuinely committed to achieving shared objectives with them. It shows you'll be a thoughtful steward of the funds.

Why it Matters

There are several specific reasons funders look for alignment when they're reading applications. An evaluation committee may read through hundreds or even thousands of applications, and alignment is one of the first ways they narrow the field. Here's what your application needs to deliver:

- Relevance: A well-aligned narrative shows that you and your project are directly relevant to the grant's purpose. You are "speaking their language," and you understand what they want to accomplish in the world. It positions you as someone they can trust to fulfill their vision and positions your proposal as a meaningful contender.

- Credibility: Alignment proves that you have thoroughly researched the funding organization and its values. This attention to detail reflects your professionalism and your credibility as a serious candidate.

- Shared Goals: When your application narrative echoes the grant's mission, it highlights that you and the funder share a common vision. This connection demonstrates a potential partnership that could extend beyond financial support. Much like online dating sites, it shows you have shared interests and may have long-term compatibility.

- Answers Their Big Question: Alignment is the main way grant reviewers evaluate how well applicants understand the grant's mission. An aligned narrative directly answers their biggest question about your project: "How will this project advance our mission?"

Alignment in Action Example

To demonstrate alignment in action, let's take a look at an example. Sarah is a visual artist who focuses on creating artwork that promotes environmental sustainability. She is looking for support for her latest art installation. The project will raise awareness of local environmental issues and will feature recycled materials sourced from the community. She is also planning to develop teaching points and curricula that can be used by the public and in classrooms. She will create a website that goes along with the installation that provides facts and tips to help solve local environmental issues.

She has identified a few potential grant opportunities, and one through The Creative Foundation stands out as a great fit for her project (this is a hypothetical organization). They are known for supporting innovative projects that bring positive change to communities through art. They also favor projects that have a teaching or educational element to them.

Here's how Sarah makes sure her grant narrative aligns with the organization's mission:

- First, Sarah thoroughly reads through the website and grant application to make sure she understands what type of projects they want to fund. In reading the materials, she **highlights values** that stand out, like they put a high value on innovation and creating positive change in the community.

- Next, she looks at **project relevance**. She writes out exactly how her project reinforces the values she highlighted. For example, she developed innovative ways of sourcing and using materials to create large art installations. She also developed an online tool that makes it easy for the public to learn more about reusing materials in their neighborhood and that drives community awareness and change.

- Turning to the application, she includes this in her impact statement to **demonstrate alignment** with their goals. She describes how her art installation will be accessible to the public and how it serves as a thought-provoking educational tool to engage the public in discussions about the local environment. In other words, she connects the dots and shows how her project directly meets their goals.

- Finally, because the organization values teaching, Sarah makes sure to include the teaching elements of her project. She may decide to add an event, such as a public workshop when the installation is complete, to reinforce community involvement and potential for change. She also highlights any previous teaching experience to demonstrate she knows how to host learning events.

With these steps, Sarah clearly draws a line connecting her project with their mission. This goes a long way toward moving her application to the next round of reviews.

Crafting an Aligned Grant Narrative

Now that we've looked at Sarah's journey, how do you follow these steps?

Research Thoroughly

Begin by thoroughly researching the funding organization. Understand its mission, its values, and its goals. Take a look at the previous grant recipients to understand the types of projects and initiatives they support. Many organizations will have these listed on their website, or you can reach out to the application contact person and ask to view a list of previous awardees. This is common practice, so they should have them available. Some organizations will even make the winning application narratives available for review. It never hurts to ask!

Highlight Overlapping Themes

Here's the meat of the work: finding alignment. Identify themes and objectives in your project that overlap with the grant's mission. Look for the things they value and where your project aligns. Whether it's promoting community engagement, creating social impact, or innovating in the field, highlight the commonalities between your work and their mission.

Use the Funder's Language

When writing the grant narrative, incorporate the same terms and language used in their grant guidelines and mission statement. This demonstrates a direct connection between your narrative and the funder's mission. Again, it shows you "speak the language" of the organization.

Going back to Sarah and her proposal, she noticed in the grant application and on the website the foundation frequently uses phrases like "community-driven initiatives," "community education," and "innovative projects." The organization clearly values community and innovation, so Sarah frames her project with these phrases. Her art installation does use innovative ways of sourcing materials, and there is a community-driven element to the work.

To mirror the organization's language, she may include a statement like:

My project is centered on developing community-driven art initiatives that align with The Creative Foundation's mission of promoting community education through innovative projects.

This isn't about making something up out of thin air. The goal is to use phrases the organization recognizes, so they can easily see how your project aligns with their mission.

Showcase Impact Alignment

In addition to mission alignment, you also need to show your project will have outcomes that align with their impact goals. Impact goals are the tangible changes the foundation aims to accomplish. For example, they might state they want to raise awareness on a certain topic, or their impact goal may be more specific, like reaching 500 schoolchildren with a particular art education program. Some foundations will state their impact goal specifically while others will be more open-ended.

For Sarah to demonstrate outcome alignment, she will need to explain how her project positively impacts the community through improved recycling education and a greater awareness of local environmental issues. She would include a statement such as:

We will track visitor traffic to the website and community workshops scheduled by local schools and community groups to measure the impact of the project. Based on foot traffic in the area and interest generated by the innovative nature of the art installation, as many as 1,000 people in the first six months will learn how to improve environmental stewardship and find new ways to recycle.

The goal is to demonstrate the positive impact your project will have, and how that directly ties to their goals.

Be Personal

It might go without saying at this point but be sure to tailor your narrative for each grant application. Your core project idea might remain the same, but your messaging should be adapted with each application to emphasize the specific aspects that best connect with each organization's mission.

Crafting a grant narrative that deeply resonates with the funder's mission requires a bit of work, but it greatly increases your chances of making it to the final rounds of evaluation (and landing those wins!).

Do the research, think strategically, and let your authentic passion for your project shine through. By showcasing a clear alignment between your project and the grant's objectives, you do more than increase your chances of success. You also position yourself as a dedicated artist who contributes meaningfully to the organization and the community. Your narrative isn't just a description of your project, it's an invitation for the funder to join you on a shared journey towards a common vision.

Tip four: Establish realistic budgets

OK, real talk: Very few artists are great with numbers and budgets. Raising my own hand on this one. But every grant will expect a project budget as part of the application. So, here's where we talk money and numbers. This section isn't just about the how; it's also about the why. It's about understanding why a realistic budget matters and how it becomes the bridge between your creativity and the practical world.

Crafting a Realistic Budget

Beyond the digits and decimal points, a budget represents the heart of your project's financial journey. It's not really about the numbers (although they're obviously important), it's about planning a route that will get your project to the finish line. Without a budget, you have no idea whether you have enough funding to complete the project, and neither will your backers.

A budget is your compass in the financial wilderness, and it ensures that your steps are measured, responsible, and aligned with your creative aspirations.

Funders want to see a realistic budget because it's a badge that shows your commitment to handling resources responsibly.

It speaks volumes about your preparedness and professionalism, and it reassures grantors that their investment will be wisely used. It also transforms your project from an artistic vision into a well-managed venture that can create change in the world.

So, how do you start this expedition? Begin by looking at each element of your project, from materials to marketing. Leave no stone unturned. List out everything you'll need to make this project a success. Do you need supplies? Travel? A researcher or an assistant to help with marketing? Do you need studio space? The more you know about what you need, the more accurately you can chart your financial course.

List everything you could possibly need. If you find out that you need to cut costs down the road, you can do that later. Right now, it's all about listing everything you need to get this project off the ground.

Once that's done and you've got a massive list of expenses, you can start to build and refine the budget:

- Define project phases. Projects usually have phases, and each section has its own budget. For an artist, a project may be divided into the creation phase, the installation or gallery phase, and the marketing phase. Each phase has different expenses associated with it, and you'll typically be requesting funds for one phase at a time. Determine which phase you're at and what you need funding for right now. You might see this called the **project scope** in applications.

- Research the costs. Take all the expenses associated with this project phase or scope and put a specific dollar amount to each item. This means getting real-world quotes, estimates, and pricing information from suppliers and service providers. Do not guess! Get actual quotes and estimates.

- Categorize the expenses. Group the expenses into categories to make it more organized and easier to understand. Common categories include things like materials, labor, marketing, travel, rentals, insurance, and equipment. There are lots of budgeting software solutions and spreadsheet templates that you can fill in if you're not sure what to include. Just search for "project budget template" to find the latest software and templates. However, it really doesn't need to be fancy. And categorizing items yourself will help you understand the true cost of your project.

- Next comes revenue sources. List all of the potential sources of income that will cover those expenses. This can include in-kind support that has already been pledged. It can include existing donations, volunteer labor, donated materials and studio space, and sales of artwork or crowdfunding efforts. You'll assign a dollar amount to each revenue source, even if it was donated or pledged as in-kind support.

- Balance the expenses and the revenue. Add up the expenses and the revenue and get them to match. They should either be the same amount, or maybe you have more revenue than expenses. If expenses outweigh revenue, go back to the drawing board. Maybe you can cut back on an area, or you can find additional assistance to cover something important. This is where you're going to figure out how much you need from granting sources, and where you need additional support.

- Write out a budget narrative. In addition to the raw budget spreadsheet, you will have space to explain each expense and its significance to the project. You don't have to explain each line item, but you can give more context to important expenses. This will help grant reviewers understand the rationale behind your budget and it gives you an opportunity to tell them why certain materials or labor are needed to make the project successful.

Overall, a realistic budget is an opportunity to demonstrate you will use the funds wisely and professionally. This gives the grant reviewers confidence that your project is well planned and it's likely to be executed successfully.

Tip five: Get in and get out

When you pick up a magazine or scroll through videos on social media, how long is your attention span? On average, you probably give 10 seconds at most before you lose interest and move on. Grant committees give slightly more attention than that to the first round of application reviews, but don't expect them to slog through pages and pages of content. Each reviewer may be looking at tens or hundreds of applications, so you've got to catch their attention, show you're relevant, and give them a reason to green light your application without wasting their time.

In other words, get in and get out. Draw them in, deliver your message succinctly, and leave a lasting impact. Here's how to keep it short while demonstrating relevance.

Clarity

Clarity is a cornerstone of effective grant applications. Being clear removes ambiguity. You want to convey the essence of your project without leaving room for confusion. Answer the big Qs:

- What is your project in one sentence?
- How will you deliver an impact?
- How does this connect with their goals?

During the first round of reviews, grant committees skim through numerous proposals. To make it to subsequent rounds of review, your proposal needs to communicate how your project is aligned with their mission as clearly and succinctly as possible. This isn't the time to be flowery or to wax philosophic on art or theory, you need to be quick and clear about how your project helps meet the organization's impact goals and mission.

Brevity

Being succinct doesn't dilute your message; it intensifies it. A concise narrative shows respect for reviewers' time and it can enhance your narrative's impact. Each word has weight, so make every word count.

When you cut all extraneous words and keep things simple, you allow your project's essence to shine through. Your grant narrative should be straightforward, factual, and conclude with a summary that leaves reviewers with a lasting impression. A clear conclusion that resonates with their mission and goals will help ensure that your proposal stays in the reviewer's mind even after they've moved on to the next application.

Your narrative should go through multiple drafts, and each draft aims to be shorter and clearer than the one before.

Precision

The art of clarity is honed through editing. Read through the narrative with a critical eye and eliminate redundancy, cut any unnecessary details, and remove jargon. Imagine your words as brushstrokes; each one should contribute to the overall image. Precision in editing is the key to creating a narrative that is both engaging and easy to comprehend. Enlist the help of a few friends to read through the narrative and point out places to cut and clarify.

A person who reads your narrative for the first time should be able to understand your mission, your project, and what you hope to accomplish without feeling bogged down by unnecessary rambling or confusing jargon. When you've accomplished that, you're good to go with submission!

Where to Find Opportunities

Directories & Resources

The following resources are a jumping off point to get you started on your funding journey. Programs and deadlines can vary each year, so always check the organization's website for the latest deadlines and information.

Americans for the Arts: ArtsU

https://artsu.americansforthearts.org

ArtsU is the educational arm of Americans for the Arts, a nonprofit organization that provides support and resources for arts programs. While many of their resources are geared toward arts institutions, some of their webinars and digital lessons are also useful for individual artists seeking funding. The news, blogs, and publications they produce can help you get the lay of the land when it comes to arts funding and how it all works. There is a membership fee to access most of their resources, but you also gain access to other professional and networking benefits with membership.

Artist Trust Resources

www.artisttrust.org/resources

Artist Trust is a nonprofit organization in Washington State, but they maintain a searchable list of national grants, jobs, residencies, and other financial opportunities that may be open to artists in other areas.

Artist Trust also awards grants and residencies to artists in Washington throughout the year, so check out their Grants webpage if you live in the state.

Candid

www.candid.org

In 2019, two of the nonprofit world's biggest organizations dedicated to research—GuideStar and Foundation Center— merged to create Candid. This is by far the largest repository of information on nonprofit organizations in the U.S.

Foundation Center was home to the most comprehensive grant and funding database in the United States, while

GuideStar was the leading resource for finding and verifying individual nonprofits. If you wanted to check tax return filings or find out if a nonprofit was legit, you'd look them up at GuideStar.

Now, as Candid, those resources are combined in one place. There is a subscription fee to access these resources, but the website provides a wealth of information on grantmaking and the social sector in general. You can also find live training and special events held across the country. If you're a student or teacher, your school may have a subscription that you can use for free. Check with your library or financial aid office to find out if there's an institutional subscription.

Visit **learning.candid.org** to access their extensive Knowledge Base, including resources and FAQs for artists and individual grantseekers.

GrantStation

www.grantstation.com

GrantStation is similar to Candid, but it is more focused on nonprofit organizations and institutions. It is included in this list because it offers webinars and courses that provide in-depth information on how to apply for grants and it also hosts a number of Canadian and international resources.

Most of the resources available at GrantStation will be above and beyond what an individual needs or can use, but there are some useful webinars that are available for free or with a one-time fee. And if you decide to make fundraising a career, this is a good place to find institutional funding ideas.

The National Assembly of State Arts Agencies (NASAA)

https://nasaa-arts.org/state-arts-agencies/saa-directory

NASAA maintains a directory of arts organizations that can be searched by region. While it only lists contact information for state-level offices (not city or county programs), it's still useful for checking different state programs, especially if you live or work in more than one state. You can also use the site to access creative economy statistics and learn more about how state governments are supporting the arts.

Federal Opportunities

These federal agencies offer grant and fellowship programs to individuals. Not all of them are arts based, but they are included here in case there is a science or teaching angle to your work-in-progress.

National Endowment for the Arts (NEA)
The NEA offers grants to support artists, arts organizations, and projects across different artistic disciplines. These grants aim to promote creativity, innovation, and artistic excellence.

Website: www.arts.gov/grants

National Endowment for the Humanities (NEH)
The NEH provides grants for individuals, scholars, and cultural institutions to support humanities-related projects, including research, exhibitions, and public programs.

Website: www.neh.gov/grants

Smithsonian Artist Research Fellowship (SARF)
This program offers artists the opportunity to conduct research at the Smithsonian Institution's museums, libraries, and archives. The fellowship supports artists in integrating the Smithsonian's collections into their creative work.

Website: www.si.edu/sarf

National Parks Arts Foundation Artist-in-Residence Program
This program offers artists the opportunity to create artwork inspired by the natural and cultural resources of national parks. Residencies provide time and space for artistic exploration within the park settings.

Website: www.nationalparksartsfoundation.org

U.S. Department of State Art in Embassies Program
The Art in Embassies Program places original works of art in U.S. embassies and consulates around the world. Artists can apply to participate in this program and have their original artwork displayed internationally.

Website: https://art.state.gov

Library of Congress Kluge Fellowship
The highly competitive Kluge Fellowship supports scholars and researchers working on digital projects that contribute to the understanding of humanities, social sciences, and fields such as architecture and law.

Website: www.loc.gov/programs/john-w-kluge-center/chairs-fellowships/fellowships/kluge-fellowships

Grants.gov
This one-stop directory and grants resource lists all available federal grants from all agencies. There are basic and advanced search features to help you find different types of grants, and the site is chock full of grant writing advice and how to apply for federal funding opportunities. Most federal grants are only available to organizations, so you may need to partner with a local nonprofit or school district to qualify.

Website: https://grants.gov

Opportunities by U.S. State

These are the ten states that award the largest amount of funding to arts projects each year. All states have some form of arts council or state arts resource, so check your state's website if it isn't listed here. These are only state-funded grants, and there may be additional regional, county or city arts funding opportunities in your area.

To find arts grants specific to your area, try searching for "arts funding" plus your city, or "arts council" and your state, city, or county. You can also check with your city hall to find out if there are any funding programs for individual artists.

Pro tip: If you live in a popular tourist area, most cities set aside some of the hotel occupancy taxes and resort taxes to be used toward supporting local artists and community projects.

As always, check each of the following websites or call their office to verify current opportunities and grant application deadlines.

California Arts Council
https://arts.ca.gov/
Application Guidelines:
https://arts.ca.gov/grants/grant-programs

New York State Council on the Arts
https://arts.ny.gov/
Application Guidelines:
https://arts.ny.gov/apply-grant

Illinois Arts Council Agency
www.arts.illinois.gov/
Application Guidelines:
www.arts.illinois.gov/grants-programs/apply

Pennsylvania Council on the Arts
www.arts.pa.gov
Application Guidelines:
www.arts.pa.gov/Pages/Apply-for-a-Grant.aspx

Texas Commission on the Arts
www.arts.texas.gov
Application Guidelines:
www.arts.texas.gov/funding/arts-response-programs

Florida Department of State, Division of Cultural Affairs
https://dos.myflorida.com/cultural
Application Guidelines:
https://dos.myflorida.com/cultural/grants/grant-programs

Massachusetts Cultural Council
https://massculturalcouncil.org
Application Guidelines:
https://massculturalcouncil.org/grants/apply-for-a-grant

Ohio Arts Council
https://oac.ohio.gov
Application Guidelines:
https://oac.ohio.gov/Grants

Michigan Council for Arts and Cultural Affairs
Website:
www.michiganbusiness.org/community/council-arts-cultural-affairs
Application Guidelines:
www.michiganbusiness.org/community/council-arts-cultural-affairs/grants

Georgia Council for the Arts
https://gaarts.org
Application Guidelines:
https://gaarts.org/grants/guidelines

Opportunities by Deadline

This is only a partial list of arts grants organized by deadline date, and there are many other opportunities available throughout the year. Grants can change each year depending on funding availability, so be sure to verify current deadlines. Some of these organizations have more than one award and more than one deadline per year.

Remember to review a grant's specific guidelines, eligibility requirements, and any additional details before applying.

January

Joan Mitchell Foundation Emerging Artist Fellowship
Application Deadline: January 14
www.joanmitchellfoundation.org

MacDowell Colony Fellowships
Application Deadline: January 15
www.macdowell.org/apply

Santa Fe Art Institute Residency
Application Deadline: January 20
https://sfai.org/

Sustainable Arts Foundation Awards
Application Deadline: January 31
www.sustainableartsfoundation.org/awards

The Hopper Prize for Visual Artists
Application Deadline: January 31
https://hopperprize.org

February

Millay Colony for the Arts
Application Deadline: February 1
www.millaycolony.org

Rauschenberg Emergency Grants
Application Deadline: February 15
https://nyfa.org

Pollock-Krasner Foundation Grant
Application Deadline: February 28
www.pkf.org/apply

Dorothea Lange-Paul Taylor Prize
Application Deadline: February 28
https://paul-taylor-prize.squarespace.com

March

Creative Capital Awards
Application Deadline: March 1
https://creative-capital.org/apply

Aaron Siskind Foundation Individual Photographer's
Fellowship
Application Deadline: March 11
www.aaronsiskind.org/grant

National Association of Latino Arts and Cultures (NALAC)
Application Deadline: March 17
www.nalac.org/apply

April

Bemis Center for Contemporary Arts Residency
Application Deadline: April 1
www.bemiscenter.org

National Endowment for the Arts Individual Fellowships
Application Deadline: April 11
www.arts.gov/grants

The Jerome Foundation Travel and Study Grant
Application Deadline: April 15
www.jeromefdn.org/apply/travel-and-study-grants

National YoungArts Foundation Awards
Application Deadline: April 29
www.youngarts.org/apply

Guggenheim Fellowship
Application Deadline: April 30
www.gf.org

May

Jerome Foundation General Program Grants
Application Deadline: May 1
www.jeromefdn.org/apply/general-program-grants

The Gottlieb Foundation Individual Support Grants
Application Deadline: May 15
www.gottliebfoundation.org/grants/individual-support-grants

Atlantic Center for the Arts Residency
Application Deadline: May 31
https://atlanticcenterforthearts.org

Ruth Lilly and Dorothy Sargent Rosenberg Poetry Fellowships
Application Deadline: May 31
www.poetryfoundation.org/foundation/prizes-fellowship

June

Creative Capital Award
Application Deadline: June 1
https://creative-capital.org

Vermont Studio Center Residency
Application Deadline: June 15
https://vermontstudiocenter.org

New York Foundation for the Arts (NYFA) Fellowship
Application Deadline: June 23
www.nyfa.org/awards-grants/artist-fellowships

John Simon Guggenheim Memorial Foundation Fellowships
Application Deadline: June 30
www.gf.org/applicants

July

The Harpo Foundation Grants for Visual Artists
Application Deadline: July 1 (deadline may vary annually)
www.harpofoundation.org/grants/grants-for-visual-artists

Djerassi Resident Artists Program
Application Deadline: July 15
https://djerassi.org

August

National YoungArts Foundation Awards
Application Deadline: August 12
www.youngarts.org/apply

The Andy Warhol Foundation Arts Writers Grant
Application Deadline: August 31
www.artswriters.org

The Elizabeth Foundation for the Arts Studio Program
Application Deadline: August 1
Website: https://www.efanyc.org/studio-program

September

Elizabeth Greenshields Foundation Grant
Application Deadline: September 1
www.elizabethgreenshieldsfoundation.org

Artadia Awards
Application Deadline: September 15
https://artadia.org

The Pollock-Krasner Foundation Fellowship
Application Deadline: September 30
https://pkf.org/

October

Anderson Ranch Arts Center Residency
Application Deadline: October 1
www.andersonranch.org

The Cintas Foundation Fellowship in Visual Arts
Application Deadline: October 1
https://cintasfoundation.org

National Sculpture Society Grants and Awards
Application Deadline: October 5
Website: https://nationalsculpture.org/grants-awards/

The Adolph and Esther Gottlieb Emergency Grant
Application Deadline: October 15
www.gottliebfoundation.org

November

Artadia Award
Application Deadline: November 1
http://artadia.org

MacDowell Colony Fellowship
Application Deadline: November 15
www.macdowell.org

The Gottlieb Foundation Individual Support Grants
Application Deadline: November 30
Website:
http://www.gottliebfoundation.org/grants/individual-support-grants/

December

Roswell Artist-in-Residence Program
Application Deadline: December 1
www.rair.org

The Gottlieb Foundation Individual Support Grants
Application Deadline: December 15
www.gottliebfoundation.org/grants

The Puffin Foundation Grant
Application Deadline: December 31
www.puffinfoundation.org/application-info

Rolling Deadlines

These grants typically have rolling application deadlines, which means they accept applications throughout the year. Be sure to check the organization's website to verify application deadlines.

The Adolph and Esther Gottlieb Emergency Grant
www.gottliebfoundation.org/emergency-grant

Artist Relief Grants
www.artistrelief.org

The Awesome Foundation Grant
www.awesomefoundation.org/apply

The Elizabeth Greenshields Foundation Grants
www.elizabethgreenshieldsfoundation.org/apply

Knight Foundation Grants
https://knightfoundation.org/programs

The Pollock-Krasner Foundation Grant
www.pkf.org/apply

Glossary

Application Deadline
The final date by which grant applications must be submitted for consideration.

Budget
A financial plan outlining estimated expenses and income for a project or program.

Fiscal Sponsorship
A relationship in which a nonprofit organization provides administrative support and financial oversight to an individual or project, allowing them to access grants.

Foundation
A nonprofit organization that provides funding to support various projects, programs, and initiatives.

Grant Proposal
A formal document outlining the purpose, goals, budget, and other details of a project to request grant funding.

In-kind Contributions
Non-monetary resources, such as goods or services, contributed to a project or program.

Letter of Inquiry (LOI)
A preliminary letter that introduces a grant seeker's project to a potential funder before submitting a full grant proposal.

Matching Funds
Funds that a grant recipient must secure from other sources to match the grant amount received.

Narrative
A compelling and structured written account within a grant proposal that describes the project's goals, purpose, approach, and anticipated outcomes. The narrative helps grant reviewers understand the project's significance and often includes storytelling elements to engage the reader.

Needs Statement
A concise description of the problem or issue a project aims to address.

Outcome
The desired result or impact that a project aims to achieve, typically linked to specific goals.

Program Officer
A staff member at a foundation responsible for managing and reviewing grant applications within a specific program area.

Project Description
A detailed explanation of the goals, activities, timeline, and expected outcomes of a proposed project.

Request for Proposal (RFP)
A formal announcement inviting organizations or individuals to submit grant proposals for a specific project or program.

Review Committee
A group of experts who evaluate grant applications and make recommendations on funding decisions.

Statement of Purpose
A concise overview of the project's objectives, purpose, and relevance to the grant program's goals.

Sustainability
The ability of a project to continue operating after grant funding ends, often demonstrated through long-term planning.

Timeline
A visual representation of project activities and their expected duration.

Unrestricted Grant
Funding that can be used by the grant recipient for general operations or programs, without specific restrictions.

Verification of Nonprofit Status
Documentation confirming an organization's legal nonprofit status, often required for grant applications.

Work Sample
Examples of an artist's previous work submitted as part of a grant application to demonstrate their skills and style.

Grants for Artists

Worksheets

Grants for Artists

CRAFTING YOUR MISSION STATEMENT

Use the following worksheet to guide you in creating your personal mission statement. Take your time and reflect on your artistic journey, values, and purpose. Be honest and authentic, and refine as needed until it accurately captures your artistic essence. This is the core of why you create!

Reflect - Write a brief summary of your artistic journey so far. Consider the themes, subjects, or mediums that have resonated with you the most. Reflect on pivotal moments or experiences that have shaped your artistic identity.

Define - Identify your core values as an artist. What beliefs and principles guide your creative process? Consider the impact you want your art to have on the world and the messages you aim to convey. Write down three to five values that are important to you.

Clarify - Define your artistic purpose. What unique perspective do you bring to your art? How do you want to make a difference through your artistic expression? Write a sentence that captures your purpose as an artist.

Example: "My purpose as an artist is to challenge societal norms and inspire introspection through thought-provoking visual narratives that evoke emotions and spark conversations."

_____

_____

_____

_____

_____

Craft - Using the reflections from the previous steps, craft a concise and authentic mission statement that encompasses your values, purpose, and artistic goals. Ensure it resonates with both art professionals and general audiences.

Example: "To create evocative and socially conscious artworks that explore the complexities of the human experience, fostering empathy, understanding, and positive change in the world."

_____

_____

_____

_____

_____

GRANT CALENDAR TEMPLATE

Use this template to create a spreadsheet or document to track grant deadlines, amounts, and contact information. You can also create calendar events on your phone and include this information in the Notes section.

MONTH: _____

Grant name:

Award history: (list date and award amount if you've won this grant before)

Amount requested:

Deadline:

Contact: (name and email/phone)

Application sent? (Y/N and date)

Awarded grant? (Y/N, date and amount)

Notes:

www.ingramcontent.com/pod-product-compliance
Lightning Source LLC
Chambersburg PA
CBHW062247290526
45794CB00006B/2437